KidLit-o Presents

The Discovery of Electricity:

A History Just for Kids

KidCaps is An Imprint of BookCaps™
www.KidLito.com

Table of Contents

About KidCaps

KidCaps is an imprint of BookCaps™ that is just for kids! Each month BookCaps will be releasing several books in this exciting imprint. Visit are website or like us on Facebook to see more!

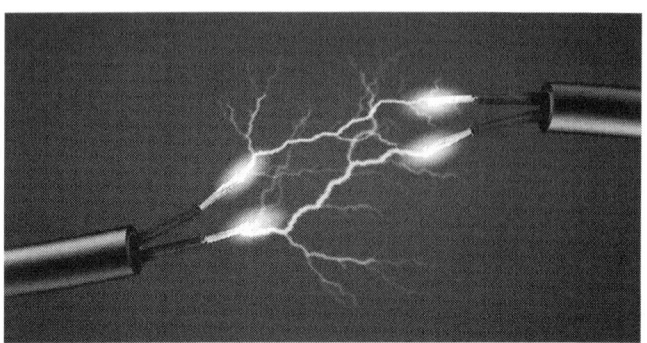

Electricity travels through wires and into our homes[1]

---

[1] Image source: http://www.planetchristmas.com/zot/

Introduction

Take a look around you–what do you see? If you are in your house, you can probably see lots of appliances, devices, and different pieces of technology. Now take a moment and count how many of those things around you need electricity to function. Don't leave any out–be sure to include ceiling fans, cell phones, computers, electronic tablets, reading lamps, air conditioners, telephones, and Wi-Fi modems. What about if you go out into your kitchen? Are there any appliances or devices there that need electricity? Of course there are! You can probably see a refrigerator, a microwave, and maybe several smaller appliances like a blender and a coffee maker and a toaster. And if you go out into the garage, you will probably see even more tools that all need to be plugged in to work, like battery chargers and door openers. It's a fact: modern homes need electricity.

But houses aren't the only buildings that need electricity. If you go into a doctor's office there will be X-Ray machines, scanners, and special monitors that all require electricity to function. Schools have bells, fire alarms, lights and phones. Police stations use radios and their cars use sirens. Even airplanes high in the sky use computers and electric motors to control their flight and to arrive safely at their destinations. During a war, soldiers use high-tech tools to see at night, to track down the bad guys hiding in the desert, and to send their bombs to the right targets.

Electricity is all around us. It gives power to the thousands of devices that make our lives easier, safer, and more organized. Electricity lets us use telephones to talk instantly with people living on the other side of the world, and lets us use computers to play video games, to watch movies, and to listen to music whenever we want. With the whole world using electricity, it can be easy to take this powerful force of nature for granted, and sometimes to even forget that it's there. After all, when was the last time you didn't have any electricity?

Sometimes we lose electrical service during a storm when powerful winds knock tree branches onto power lines. Has that ever happened to you? Did you feel strange when you didn't have any electricity in your house? What did it feel like when you had to sit there in the dark with no TV, no music, and no internet? The power company usually fixes any problems quickly, but electricity has become such an important part of our lives that can be difficult to imagine going even a few hours without using something powered by electricity. But when was the last time you thought about where all that electricity comes from, and how it got to be so popular?

In this book, we will be looking at the discovery of electricity. We will talk a little about the science of what electricity is, and then we will talk about how it was discovered and how smart inventors found a way to use this force to make the world a more comfortable place to live in. What would you like to learn about electricity?

This book will look at the discovery of electricity from six different angles.

It will start by talking about what led up to the discovery of electricity. The basic principle of electrical charge was known by both the ancient Egyptians and Greeks, but it wasn't until the 1700s and 1800s that researchers were able to discover what caused electrical charges and how those charges could be used to create new technology. This first section will show you who made some of those important discoveries and how the discoveries were used to design new devices and appliances.

Next, you will learn a little more about *why* electricity was invented–in other words, *why* were scientists so interested in electricity and in the positive and negative charges that it carried. We will see how the desire to learn more about the world and to progress motivated scientists for decades, and we will also learn about the scientific method that they used to test and prove their theories.

Then we will see more of what happened during the exciting times of the late 1800s and early 1900s, when the true power of electricity was harnessed, and inventors like Samuel Morse, Alfred Vail, Thomas Edison, George Westinghouse, and Alexander Graham Bell began to show the world what could be done with this powerful force. We will see some of the competition between the inventors trying to sell their products and how electricity began to be manufactured on a large scale and distributed across the country.

The next section will tell us what it was like to be a kid back then. You will have the opportunity to imagine what life was like as new discoveries literally changed the world around you. You will see how electricity changed the way that people communicated, the way they worked, and even the way that they had fun.

Then we will see how the greatest discoveries of electricity came to an end. What did all of the hours spent studying this exciting new force lead to? We will have a look at how the world changed since the discovery of electricity, and how the world that we live in today would be different if it weren't for the hard work of scientists and researchers living over a hundred years ago.

The discovery of electricity was a big moment in the world of science. But unlike other important discoveries, the discovery of electricity was mainly used to make the world a better place. As you read through this book, try to imagine what you would have thought about all this exciting science, and what you would have done if you had been alive. Would you have encouraged the researchers to continue with their experiments or would you have told them to stop spending so much time in their laboratories? Would you have tried to find a way to use electricity to make the world a better place or just as a way to get rich?

The discovery of electricity did not happen overnight, and it took lots of hard work and long hours to get us to where we are today. This book will help you to appreciate that the comfortable life that we have today is only possible because smart people throughout the years were willing to look a little closer at the world around them to try and understand it better.

Chapter 1: What Led Up to the Discovery of Electricity?

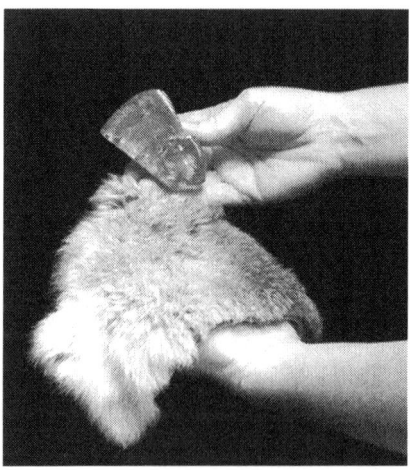

The ancient Greeks rubbed amber and cat fur together to produce static electricity[2]

What sets aside great thinkers like Benjamin Franklin from the rest of us? Well, great thinkers have the ability to see exceptional things that the rest of us fail to notice. Although some basic principles of electricity were known for years, it wasn't until some great thinkers arrived later in time and began to see how exceptional this force of nature really was.

How much do you know about electricity? Let's take a quick moment to talk about what it is, and then we will see how several smart people discovered the power of this natural force.

[2] Image source: http://onlinephys.com/faraday.html

As you may have learned in school, everything around us is made up of atoms. Atoms, in turn, are made up of three particles called protons, neutrons, and electrons. The protons and neutrons always stick together in the center of the atom (in an area called the "nucleus"). The electrons, on the other hand, zip around the nucleus, orbiting it in several layers called "shells". In each atom, the protons have a slightly positive charge, the electrons have a slightly negative charge, and the neutrons have no charge at all.

Most atoms have the same number of protons, neutrons, and electrons making them up. For example, an atom of the metal zinc has thirty electrons, thirty protons, and thirty neutrons. An atom of oxygen, on the other hand, has eight electrons, eight protons, and eight neutrons. The fact that each atom has the same number of negative and positive charges in it means that the atom as a whole has neither a positive nor negative charge.

Although lots of protons and neutrons can be clumped together in the nucleus, too many electrons can't be in the same place. For that reason, electrons spread themselves out in several layers (shells) around the nucleus. But something strange happens: electrons almost always organize themselves into layers with the same amount of electrons on each shell. For example, there are always up to two electrons on the first shell, up to eight electrons on the second shell, up to eighteen electrons on the third shell, and so on.

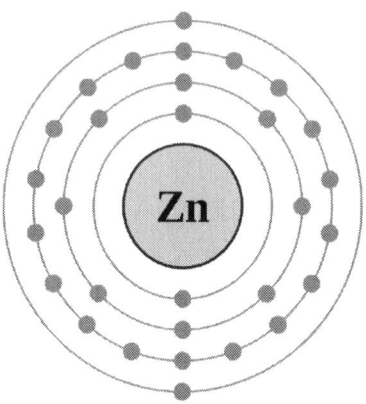

An atom of zinc has thirty electrons arranged into four shells of 2, 8, 18, and 2[3]

As atoms get close to each other, these electrons often start to interact. Sometimes two atoms share electrons and become a molecule (like when two atoms of hydrogen get together with an atom of oxygen and form a molecule of water- H_2O). Electrons genuinely like to move around in atoms of metal elements (like copper), and, in fact, the electrons will sometimes jump from one atom to another. This means that even though metal seems strong, the electrons are not as stable as in other materials.

It is this movement of electrons from one atom to another that is the basis for electricity. Like water flowing through a pipe, the flow of electrons through atoms of metal is referred to as a current. For a long time, the flow of electricity was more of a party trick

[3] Image source: http://upload.wikimedia.org/wikipedia/commons/c/c5/Electron_sh ell_030_Zinc_-_no_label.svg

than an essential part of daily life. Ancient peoples, like the Greeks and the Egyptians, had been able to observe some strange things in nature, like lightning, magnets, and static electricity, but it didn't seem like there was going to be any real way to use these strange observations. The Egyptians knew that some species of eels could produce electric current, and so they used a word related to lightning to describe these eels. This shows us that the ancient Egyptians were able to associate lighting and electricity from a early time.

The Greeks, on the other hand, would rub a piece of amber stone against cat fur (as you can see in the picture at the beginning of this section). What would happen when they rubbed the amber against the fur? A small electrical charge would build up on the amber, and the charged amber would attract light objects, like feathers, to it.

The small charge on a piece of amber was interesting to look at, but it hardly seemed like something that was going to change the world. But in 1660, when he was trying to understand more about the movement of the stars, German scientist Otto von Guericke designed a machine that rotated a ball of sulfur against a pad inside of a glass jar. When he put his hand against the ball later, Otto von Guericke could hear a crackling and could see small sparks flying. He had just taken a step towards understanding electricity, and how to create it: he had discovered that static electricity could be made with a variety of materials.

Benjamin Franklin, who lived during the next century, was impressed with the power of lightning, and he suspected that small sparks of static electricity and huge bolts of lightning in the sky might be related. So he started doing several experiments during thunderstorms. Scientists in Europe had already discovered how to store small electrical charges inside of bottles called "Leyden jars", and so Ben Franklin figured that if lightning and electricity were related then he should be able to capture some electricity from the air during a lightning storm and store it in his jar. On one stormy day in 1752, Ben Franklin went outside with his son to test his theory.

He flew a kite into the air using a silk string, and tied a metal key to the bottom of the string. A small piece of metal wire connected the key to a nail in the top of a Leyden jar. As the thunderstorm moved closer and static electricity began to fill the air, Benjamin Franklin went into a nearby barn with his son so as not to get rained on. After the storm had passed, Ben Franklin moved his hand near the key and received quite a shock. What had happened? Electricity from the air during the storm had travelled down the string to the iron key and been collected into the jar. It was this electricity that had shocked Ben Franklin when he got too close to the key that was connected to it. Ben Franklin had just proved that lightning and electricity were the same thing. The force generated by Otto von Guericke, the ancient Greeks, and some eels in Egypt was the same force that lit up the sky during a thunderstorm.

Benjamin Franklin proved that lightning is actually electricity[4]

It was a dangerous thing for Ben Franklin to do, to carry out that experiment, but it fascinated scientists everywhere. Not long after Ben Franklin's experiment, Italian scientist Alessandro Volta designed the first battery. Instead of using motion or lighting to capture electricity, he decided to find a way to make electricity. He put several pieces of metal one on top of the other and noted how the flow of electrons from one piece to the next, and when the two ends of the pile were connected it produced an electric current. Alessandro Volta had just created the world's first battery, and in his honor we now measure electricity in *volts*.

Scientists around the world were amazed to see that something as powerful as lightning could be caused by something that couldn't even be seen, like an

---

[4] Image source: http://www.britannica.com/EBchecked/media/15462/Benjamin-Franklins-experiment-proving-the-identity-of-lightning-and-electricity

electron. But there was still some confusion about how magnets were related to electricity. It was noticed that compass needles were affected by electrical currents. Michael Faraday, an English scientist, helped to clear that up in in 1821, when he used a rotating magnet to generate electrical current. It was learned that magnetism and electricity are actually closely related and that you can't have one without the other. In fact, scientists today often refer to the "electromagnetic force" when talking about physics.

It was about this time that electricity stopped being something fascinating only to scientists. Inventors and engineers started to race to find practical applications for electricity and to find ways of using it to make the world a better place. One of the earliest uses of electricity was in the field of communication. In Europe scientists experimented with ways of using electrical currents to communicate. They tried sending pulses that would change letters on a box on the other end. In fact, in Great Brittani police used one such message to catch a criminal by describing his appearance! But in 1836, American inventor Samuel Morse devised a simple code and a way of transmitting it using electricity and simple wires. Using powerful electromagnets made by fellow inventor Alfred Vail, these signals could be sent for long distances, even on low quality wires. Within a few decades, everyone was using the electric telegraph and Morse code to send messages from one side of the country to the other. Abraham Lincoln even used telegraph lines to direct the movements of his troops during the Civil War. It wasn't long before telegraph cables were laid across the floor of the Atlantic Ocean to send telegrams to and from Europe.

One of the most important uses of electricity, and one that made everyone everywhere wants access to it was the invention of the light bulb. American scientist Thomas Edison, in 1879, helped to improve the design of a small light bulb for everyday use, and the world loved it. For the first time, a light bulb was designed that could be burned for many hours, and that didn't require a lot of electricity to use.

The basic principles of electricity were finally beginning to be understood, and some smart people were finding ways of using those principles to make the world a better place.

Chapter 2: Why Was Electricity Discovered?

Have you ever woken up in the middle of the night and tried to walk around your bedroom? It's not always easy, even in a place that you are familiar with. Now imagine what it would be like to try and walk around in pitch black at a friend's house, where you aren't so familiar with the layout of the room. In a way, scientists working with electricity down through the years have been walking around in the dark. After all, they can't see atoms or their electrons, so it is not as easy to find out what is going on. How did they learn so much about electricity if they couldn't see the atoms or electrons? They used the scientific method.

Do you remember the example we used of walking around in the dark in a friend's house? How would you solve that problem? First, you would need to identify the problem, think about it, try out a couple of ideas, and then see what the results were. For example, you might start by trying to find the light switch. You would probably think about where you have seen light switches in other houses, and then you could look for it with your hand. If you were wrong, you could try again.

Scientists working with electricity would use this same basic method to learn. Look at the following picture of the Scientific Method:

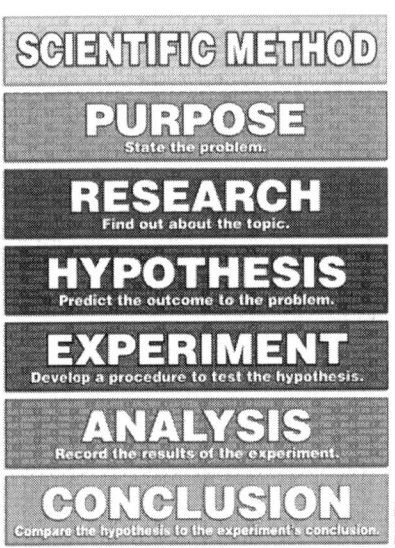

The Scientific Method is a series of steps to solve problems and to learn more about the universe[5]

Year by year, scientists would get ready for the next step in learning about electricity. They would decide what the next step should be, they would research it, they would form a theory, and then they would experiment until they got the result they wanted. It was a lot of work, but little by little the world started to understand how all objects were made up of little atoms with electrons, and that these electrons created an electrical charge whenever they moved.

But what kept these hardworking scientists motivated throughout the years? Why didn't they just give up

---

[5] Image source: http://conversiongarden.com/tag/scientific-method/

when things looked too difficult or when their experiments didn't turn out the way they wanted?

It was the desire to **learn** and the desire to help the world to **progress** that kept them motivated.

While most people are happy to just work in their jobs and to quietly raise a family, there have always been some extraordinary people through the centuries who have tried to see the big picture. Instead of thinking only of themselves, they think about the entire human race. It is this way of thinking that still motivates scientists today who are continuing to tell us more about the planet, the solar system, and the entire universe around us.

But what those scientists do with the information is what makes them really special. Especially in the case of electricity, we see these astounding discoveries being used to help make the world a better place. From the very beginning, electricity was used to make people happy. Think about the telegraph. The electric telegraph was used to help people to stay in touch with each other. True, Abraham Lincoln did use it for a short time to fight a war, but mostly it was used to help old friends to stay in touch, to help people living far away keep up to speed on current events, and to help countries to solve their problems and to avoid fighting big wars if at all possible.

Most scientists working with electricity were motivated by these pure causes, wanting to learn and to make the world a better place. However, there were some other scientists and inventors, like Thomas Edison, who also tried to make some money by selling to the public the new technology made possible by electricity. While it is not necessarily a bad idea to try and make money from science or inventions, it can change the way that scientists go about researching and experimenting. For example, we will see in the next section how Thomas Edison became competitive with George Westinghouse and started a sort of "war" with him. In that case, technological competition brought out the worst in those involved.

Thankfully, most of the scientists who worked to bring us the modern miracle of electricity were dedicated to learning as much as they could and to sharing that knowledge with the world. Because of their hard work and determination, we have an entire world that is so much better because of electricity.

Chapter 3: What Happened During the Discovery of Electricity?

A worker high above New York City adds a piece of metal to a building under construction[6]

The same way builders construct a skyscraper one floor at a time, many scientists over the years each took small steps towards the discovery of electricity. The Greeks and Egyptians discovered static electricity, Benjamin Franklin confirmed that lightning was a powerful electric charge, and Alessandro Volta created the first working battery using pieces of metal stacked one on top of the other. By the time Thomas Edison was born, people were

[6] Image source: http://ephemeralnewyork.wordpress.com/tag/skyscrapers-of-new-york-city/

using electricity to send messages to each other, to power small motors, and in some cases even to treat patients in hospitals. But the time had come to see what electricity actually could do to make the world a better place.

The telegraph was making communication easier, but many inventors were sure that this newly discovered force of nature could do even more to help mankind. Several inventors had already designed small bulbs that could provide light. These bulbs were called "incandescent lights". How were they made?

Inventors would suck all of the air out of a small glass bulb using a pump (thus creating vacuum) and then they would pass an electrical current through a piece of material inside the sealed glass. The material would heat up and start glowing, but because there was no air inside the bulb no fire could break out. The first light bulbs were better than candles, but they too dim to be used outside or in large factories, so they were only used indoors in small spaces.

By the 1870s, a new form of lighting had been developed: arc lighting. This used two pieces of metal set slightly apart from each other. When enough electrical current passed through the bulbs, the electrons in one piece of metal would jump through the vacuum to the other piece, creating an "arc" (which looks like a tiny lightning bolt). These arc lamps burned more brightly then the incandescent bulbs did, and were quickly installed outdoors in public areas and in large factories and train stations.

In fact, they were so bright that they weren't suited for use in homes.

Each of these powerful lamps needed their own large battery (or several batteries) to produce enough light. What Thomas Edison decided to do was to create a better light bulb but also to design and build a method of generating and transporting electricity for public use. He imagined a world where everybody would have access to electricity in their homes, and that it would not be something that only rich people and large companies could afford to have.

Edison decided to focus on a system Direct Current (DC) electricity would be provided to homes and businesses around the country. He devised a whole system where a generator would create the electricity, which would then be sent out to the homes and business that were in the area. In case there were any problems with the generator, large storage batteries would continue to send electricity out while the problem was fixed. But Thomas Edison had a special reason for wanting to make sure that everyone used his DC electricity: he had many patents protecting DC technology. If anyone wanted to use DC electricity, Edison would get at least some of the money they made. So can you imagine how Edison felt when George Westinghouse offered the world a different way of producing and distributing electricity?

George Westinghouse felt that the DC electrical distribution system had too many flaws. For example, he felt that, over long distances, a lot of the power would be lost. So he decided to try to improve another method that had been developed and to promote it as the best way: Alternating Current (AC) electricity. The main difference was that there were no batteries and that the current could be sent for much longer distances, meaning a power plant could be located far away from the houses that it gave electricity to. Also, more power could be sent over the wires used for distribution, which meant that fewer power plants would need to be built and maintained, making AC electricity even cheaper and available to more people.

Thomas Edison was not happy with the idea of George Westinghouse convincing people to choose AC electricity distribution instead of DC. At the end of the day, it would mean less money in Edison's pocket. So what did Edison do? He decided to start a "War of Currents" to convince the world that DC electricity was better than AC electricity. How did he do it?

Edison began to travel to several big cities and to tell people that Westinghouse's AC electricity was unsafe. He would even gather up stray animals and electrocute them with AC electricity to prove his point. He even went so far as to electrocute an elephant named Topsy on January 4, 1903. The elephant had attacked several people, and its owners decided that it must be killed. Thomas Edison took advantage of the situation to kill the elephant with (and to film the killing using a video camera) by sending 6,600 volts of electricity through its body.

The animal fell to the ground and died quickly, and Edison's competitors were shocked that he would go so far to prove his point.

But that wasn't the only kind of death that Thomas Edison helped to make possible during the War of Currents.

Even though he was against the death penalty, Edison was convinced that his system of DC electricity must be used by everyone and that no one should use AC electricity. In 1890, he decided that using AC electricity to kill criminals would make the whole world think that AC electricity was too dangerous to use. It would convince them that DC was the best way to go. On August 6, 1890, a criminal named William Kemmler was executed in New York using an electric chair designed by Harold P. Brown (an employee of Edison). This chair sent 2,000 volts of electricity through his body, and it took about 8 minutes to kill him. Everyone was shocked at how cruel death by electric chair seemed to be.

The War of Currents was getting nasty.

By the late 1890s, AC power was starting to get more popular and to become more respected in the eyes of many scientists. George Westinghouse installed a power plant in Niagara Falls to use the water pressure to generate electricity and send it to consumers. In 1892, General Electric, formed using Edison's technology, decided to ignore Edison's ideas and pursue AC power. Even though Edison himself kept trying to protect his patents and ideas, he soon found himself fighting practically alone.

The world had decided without him to move ahead with AC power.

Electricity was no longer just a party trick; it was the future.

Chapter 4: What Was It Like to Be a Kid Back Then?

Kids using an electric telegraph[7]

Can you imagine what it was like to be a kid back when electricity was being discovered and put to use for the first time? Well, let's first have a look at what life was like before electricity was discovered and made popular, and then at what your life would have been like around the year 1900, when electricity was starting to appear in many homes and businesses across the country.

Before electricity was discovered and made popular, people depended a lot more on the sun than we do today. In fact, the movement of the sun helped them to make their schedule each day. People could only work outside when the sun was out; otherwise they couldn't see what they were doing. Also, folks didn't

[7] Image source: http://www.itu.int/wtisd/2011/initiatives.html

like to travel at night because it just wasn't safe. They were worried that they might trip on the road or that they might be hurt by an animal or a mugger. So unless the sun was out, most people stayed inside their homes. But what would they do inside their homes if they weren't tired enough ot go to sleep?

Before they had electricity in their homes, most people needed candles and lanterns to see when walking around and spending time inside their house. On nights when it got dark early, families would often spend time together gathered around a fire or a candle and talking, reading, sewing, playing with toys, or even playing musical instruments and singing together. In most families, there were only one or two lamps, so in order to share the light everyone had to get together in the same room.

Can you imagine spending so much time with your family? Today, families using electrical devices often separate from each other. The kids might go play videogames on the computer or chat online in one room, dad might watch TV in another room, and mom might surf online or read an eBook in a third room. But back then, families were forced to spend more time together. What was the result? Without electricity, many families found that they actually kind of enjoyed each other's company. They liked laughing together, singing together, and talking together.

When electricity was discovered, and inventors like Thomas Edison and Alexander Graham Bell began to design light bulbs, distribution networks, telephones, record players, radios, and movies, life changed for the average kid living in the United States. He began to spend more time out of the house than inside it. Streets had electric lights; there were movie theatres in many cities, and there were lights and radios in many houses. Families started to spend less time talking and more time doing other things. Because of the lights in their houses, people stayed up later, and they spent more time having fun individually instead of as a family.

Now imagine what it was like to see the War of Currents, fought mainly between Thomas Edison and George Westinghouse. Can you imagine hearing about Thomas Edison hurting animals to prove a point? Would you have agreed with that or would you have thought that Edison had gone too far? But, on the other hand, wouldn't it have been exciting to hear that George Westinghouse built a generator and was making electricity using the water of Niagara Falls?

As a kid, you would have been among the first people in the world to be a part of the new technology made possible by electricity. Do you think that you would have realized how important these discoveries were or would you have been too busy playing to take notice? Would you have tried to keep up with the scientists as they talked in the newspapers about new types of inventions, or would you have gotten bored?

The discovery of electricity changed the world. It let people communicate over long distances, have fun watching movies and listening to music, and work longer hours and feel safer on the streets. The world was a lot better for most people after electricity was discovered and put to use. If you had been a kid back then, you would have gotten to see history happen right before your eyes.

Chapter 5: How Did the Discovery of Electricity Come to An End?

Once the biggest companies decided that AC power was the way to go, there wasn't a lot more to discover about electrical power itself. Many scientists had worked hard to understand the math behind it all, so what people were most interested in was how to put all of that knowledge to good use. In other words, how could electricity be used to make the world a better place?

Samuel Morse and Alfred Vail had gotten the ball rolling with their invention of the electric telegraph, which could send messages to people living on the other side of the world. In 1876, Alexander Graham Bell found that a person's voice could be changed into an electrical signal and be transmitted like a telegraph to another device, which would turn it back into sound. He soon made the world's first telephone. In 1892, he made a long distance phone call from New York to Chicago, and in 1915, he called his assistant Thomas Watson across the country in San Francisco from New York.

Alexander Bell called Chicago from New York in 1892[8]

It wasn't long before there were phone calls being made all over the world.

In the meantime, inventors began to use certain waves produced by electricity to send signals. They discovered that these waves could be sent long distances to special devices that would be used to interpret the message carried by the waves. These waves, created by electricity, soon came to be known as radio waves. They were installed on ship for emergency telegraph communication, but soon people were using them to broadcast music, religious programming, news, and entertainment shows in cities around the country. Because radios couldn't broadcast too far, each city would play different shows and programs, although some national networks would buy stations in each area to play similar programs.

But scientists weren't done with electricity yet.

Now that AC power was everywhere, it was decided that it should be used for more than lighting and entertainment; it should be used in factories to power machines. One of the most important inventions was the AC motor. This motor, when it had a current of electricity, could be used to move all kinds of machines. This ability to move large machines using electricity is part of what led to something called the Second Industrial Revolution, a time when factories were built all around the world and countries began to produce more goods than ever.

One of the things that made electricity special was that it was something that could be produced anytime, anywhere. Unlike many natural elements that were needed for technology and progress, there was never going to be an end to the supply of electricity. Think about it: eventually it will be hard to find elements like gold, copper, and iron in the earth. There is only so much that we can dig up. The same is even true to a certain degree with wood: if we cut down the trees faster than they can grow, eventually we will have no more trees left. But that is not the case with electricity. Whether the generator is moved by water, by wind, or by nuclear power, we will never run out of electricity.

This makes electricity one of the most exciting discoveries in history. It is a source of energy that can be used by people everywhere, and it will never disappear. The world changed almost overnight because of electricity. People went from living quiet, almost isolated lives to being connected with practically the entire world. Instead of only spending time with family members and a few neighbors, suddenly they were being entertained through their radios by strangers living on the other side of the country, doing business with people living in other lands, and establishing one American culture that stretched across the entire country. The United States were becoming closer than ever before.

Chapter 6: What Happened After the Discovery of Electricity?

While most of the science behind electricity was understood by the time the 1900s began, what still wasn't known is how it would be used next. In fact, even today there is a lot of attention given to new inventions and ways of using electricity. There are still inventors like George Westinghouse, Alexander Graham Bell, and Thomas Edison who want to make the world a better place using electricity.

For example, did you know that there are people currently producing cars that use electricity to move, instead of gasoline, thus reducing pollution? Did you know that there are ways of using the panels on the roof of your house to capture sunlight and generate electricity that way? And think for a moment about how computers and the internet have changed the way that we live each day of our life.

Thanks to computers and the internet, people can now work from anywhere in the world. They can go to a coffee shop, rent an office, or even stay at home and still work for a boss. People can share videos and messages online, and they can even attend college courses from the comfort of their living room. The internet also lets governments stay in touch with their soldiers, and lets heads of countries communicate with each other and in many cases avoid turning small misunderstandings in epic wars.

There are even people who want to try and take it a step further. There are inventors who want to find a way to put humans and computers together. In other words, they want to put our thoughts, emotions, and personality onto the internet, as a way for people to live forever and never die. Do you like that idea or does it kind of scare you and sound a little weird?

In the beginning of this book, you were asked to look around you and to count all the devices and appliances that use electricity. How many did you count? Five? Ten? Fifteen? More? Our daily life would be different if it weren't for electricity and all the technology it has made possible. Some people today try to challenge themselves to see if they can live an entire day without using electricity. From the time they wake up until the moment they go to bed they try to go an entire day without using a phone, a computer, turning on any lights, opening the fridge, or using the microwave. Do you think you could do something like that? Would it help you to appreciate how big a part electricity plays in your daily life and how much you take it for granted sometimes?

Since electricity was discovered, most of the changes it has brought on the world have been good. However, like everything that humans do, sometimes even a great discovery (like electricity) can bring some problems with it. What kind of bad things has the discovery of electricity brought into the world?

One of the major problems has to do with how the electricity is generated. As we saw, electricity can be generated using water (like at Niagara Falls) or even using solar panels installed on rooftops. But many power companies want to create more electricity quickly. Sometimes, these methods that they have used have dangerous side effects. For example, some companies turn their electrical generators using steam. There is a big pot of water that boils and the steam, as it rises, turn turbines (propeller blades) and magnets inside the turbine generate electricity. But what do some of these companies use to heat up the water? Some power companies have built plants that burn coal and others have built plants that use nuclear rods to heat up the water. But what's the problem?

Burning coal releases lots of pollution into the air and groundwater. It is estimated that over one million people per year have their lives shortened because of the chemicals released through burning coal. Also, huge pieces of land are destroyed to get to the coal, which is buried deep underground. Sometimes these coal mines collapse, trapping the miners inside.

Nuclear plants have problems of their own. Sometimes the nuclear reactions that heat up the water get out of control and the reactors explode. This happened in the United States at the Three Mile Island nuclear plant, and in Ukraine, at the Chernobyl nuclear plant. But even if everything goes according to plan, large amounts of highly radioactive material is produced by these plants, and no one really knows what to do with the radioactive material once they are done using it. Some nuclear plants have tried to store the waste underground, but one plant that did that (in Washington, USA) soon discovered that the material was leaking out and polluting the groundwater near the plant.

We can be happy when se see smart people try to make sure that generating electricity doesn't harm the planet or the people living on it. For example, along with solar panels, did you know that there are other ways of generating electricity that don't require coal or nuclear power? In some countries, they use giant fans blades that spin around in the wind and use the motion to generate electricity.

But there is even more exciting technology planned. Right now, scientists are trying to design a way to generate electricity using underwater turbines. Just like fan blades that use the wind to spin and generate electricity, these underwater turbines (fans) will spin as the tides more past them, pulled back and forth every day by the gravity of the moon. Because water is thicker than air, each turn will be stronger and will generate more electricity. The best part is that these underwater turbines will not generate harmful pollution and will not endanger any animals (unlike aboveground turbines, which often kill large numbers of birds each year).

The same type of creative people that helped to discover electricity and capture its power are now looking for ways to produce it without harming the earth. They want humans to be able to enjoy a comfortable life without ruining their home.

Conclusion

What an fascinating book! We have learned so much about the discovery and use of electricity. What was your favorite part? Let's review the main of points of each section before we finish.

We started by talking about what led up to the discovery of electricity. The basic principles of electrical charges were discovered by the ancient Egyptians and Greeks, but it wasn't until the 1700s and 1800s that researchers were able to discover what caused the electrical charges and how they could be used in technology. People like Benjamin Franklin, Alessandro Volta, and Thomas Edison tried to understand more about how electricity worked. They also tried to find a way to use it to make the world a better place. But they had to develop new technologies and new ideas in order to make it work.

Next, we learned a little more about *why* electricity was invented–in other words, *why* were scientists so interested in electricity and in the positive and negative charges that it carried. It was the desire to learn more about the world and a desire to progress that motivated scientists for decades. We saw how they used the scientific method to test out theories and to learn more about tiny particles that they couldn't even see. We can be thankful that these intelligent people didn't give up along the way, even though it wasn't always easy.

Then we saw more of what happened during the exciting times of the late 1800s, when the true power of electricity was harnessed, and inventors like Thomas Edison and George Westinghouse began to show the world what could be done with this powerful force. It was exciting to see inventions like the telegraph the telephone, the radio, and the video camera be developed and put to use. But we all saw the darker side of the discovery of electricity: the competition between the inventors trying to sell their products. Do you remember how George Westinghouse and Thomas Edison each tried to sell their technology and their way of doing things? It was sad to see Thomas Edison go to such great lengths to prove his point, even killing animals in front of large crowds.

The next section told us what it was like to be a kid back then. You had the opportunity to imagine what life was like as new discoveries literally changed the world around you. We imagined what it was like to be alive when electricity was first being discovered. Did you like how people lived back then, quiet lives focused on family? Or did you like the action and excitement that came with the development of new technology? We saw how electricity changed the way that people communicated, the way they worked, and even the way they had fun,

Finally, we saw how the major discoveries of electricity came to an end. By the start of the 1900s, most of the science and math behind electricity was understood. We saw how since then, the focus has been on finding new ways to generate the electricity and to use it to make life more comfortable and more interesting. There can be no doubt: the world that we live in today would be different if it weren't for the hard work of scientists and researchers living over a hundred years ago.

The discovery of electricity has been an exciting journey to follow. We have seen that the curiosity of a few individuals was enough to see something amazing, something that nobody else saw. And it has made possible so many good things in the world. What about you? What will you do with your curiosity?

Some people are like Thomas Edison. They may be smart, and they may want to learn about the world, but often they are willing to listen to other people's suggestion and they even try to keep other people from getting ahead. How much better to be like other inventors, who shared what they learned with the world and kept the big picture in mind! Instead of focusing just on the money that they could make with their new discoveries, they thought about what was the best thing to do to help everybody. Like a team of builders working on a skyscraper, they were able to each contribute a piece and help make something incredible.

There are still a lot of discoveries to make out there, and maybe someday scientists will find something even better than electricity to use. But there are still lots of ways that we can make the world better right now today. Did you know that 25% of the world population still doesn't have access to electricity? That means that one out of every four people can't use a computer or turn on the lights whenever they want. Will you be part of the solution, part of the team that helps everyone have access to this important utility?

Also, we still need to find a better way to make electricity, one that doesn't harm the earth so much. Will you try to use your imagination to find a better solution? The world would be a better place if you did.

In history, there are a few moments that change everything else after them. When Benjamin Franklin flew his kite during an electrical storm, when Alessandro Volta made the first battery, and when Alexander Graham Bell made the first telephone call, they each made discoveries that changed the world. You can do the same thing, if you never lose your curiosity and your desire to learn.

12032323R00026

Printed in Great Britain
by Amazon.co.uk, Ltd.,
Marston Gate.